Nature's
Wonders

Published by
Two-Can Publishing
A Division of Zenith Entertainment plc
43–45 Dorset Street
London W1H 4AB

First published by Two-Can Publishing in 2000
© Two-Can Publishing, 2000
© Text Jenny Wood, 1990, 1991

COVER
Photographs courtesy of Planet Earth/Eastcott & Momatiuk(iceberg),
Planet Earth/David A. Ponton (temperate rainforest),
Michael Dunning (lava/Hawaii) and Paul or Lindamarie Ambros
(lightning), Telegraph Colour Library

VOLCANOES
Author and Editor: Jenny Wood; Design: Claire Legemah
Photographic credits: GeoScience Features Picture Library: p.7;
GeoScience Features Picture Library: pp.8-9; Explorer: p.9; Frank
Lane Picture Agency Ltd: p.10 (inset); Explorer: pp.10-11; Frank
Lane Picture Agency Ltd: p.12 (top); Bruce Coleman: p.12 (bottom);
Robert Harding Picture Library: p.13 (left); GeoScience Features
Picture Library: p.13 (right); Zefa: p.16; GeoScience Features
Picture Library: p.17; Zefa: p.18 (both); Survival Anglia Photo
Library: p.20; Rex Features: p.21 (top); GeoScience Features Picture
Library: p.21 (bottom); The Hutchinson Library: p.21 (right);
Explorer: p.22; Zefa: pp.24-25; Ardea: p.24 (inset); Survival Anglia
Photo Library: p.25 (left inset); Zefa: p.25 (right inset)
Illustration credits: Francis Mosley: pp.6, 7, 9, 14, 15, 16, 19, 23;
Linden Artists/Malcolm Stokes: pp.26–30

ICEBERGS
Author and Editor: Jenny Wood; Design: Claire Legemah
Photographic credits: Arctic Camera: pp.34-35; Frank Lane Picture
Agency Ltd: p.36; Robert Harding Picture Library: p.37 (top); Planet
Earth Pictures: p.37 (bottom); Frank Lane Picture Agency Ltd: p.38,
p.39 (left inset); Eric & David Hosking: p.39 (right inset); The
Hutchinson Library: p.39 (main picture), p.40; Robert Harding
Picture Library: p.41; Zefa: p.42; Ardea: p.43; Eric & David
Hosking: pp.44-45; Frank Lane Picture Agency Ltd: p.46; Ardea:
p.47 (top); Survival Anglia Photo Library: p.47 (bottom); Planet
Earth Pictures: p.48 (inset); Charles Swithinbank: pp.48-49;
Survival Anglia Photo Library: p.50 (top); Bryan and Cherry
Alexander: p.50 (bottom); Survival Anglia Photo Library: p.52;
Zefa: p.53 (top); British Antarctic Survey: p.53 (bottom);
Illustration credits: Francis Mosley: pp.35, 36, 37, 41,
43, 45, 51, 52; Grahame Corbett: pp.54–58

JUNGLES
Author: Jenny Wood; Editor: Claire Watts; Consultant: Roger
Hammond, Director of Living Earth; Design: Claire Legemah
Photographic credits: Ardea: p.63, p.66 (top); Bruce Coleman: p.66
(bottom), p.67 (top); Survival Anglia: p.67 (bottom); Frank Lane:
p.68 (top & bottom); Survival Anglia: p.69; Bruce Coleman:
p.70 (top & bottom); Hutchinson: p.71; Frank Lane:
p.72 (top & bottom), p.73 (top & bottom); Hutchinson: p.74;
Survival Anglia: p.75 (top & bottom); Hutchinson: p.76, p.77;
Oxford Scientific Films: p.78; Planet Earth
Pictures: p.80; Mark Edwards: p.81
Illustration credits: Francis Mosley: pp.62-81, p.87;
Linden Artists/Jon Davis: pp.82-86

STORMS
Author and Editor: Jenny Wood; Design: Claire Legemah
Photographic credits: Tony Stone Associates Ltd: p.91; Robert
Harding Picture Library: p.92; Zefa: p.93 (top); The Meteorological
Office/ETH Zurich: p.93 (bottom); Science Photo Library/Bruce
Coleman: p.95 (inset); Zefa: p.96; Explorer: pp.96-97; Tony Stone
Associates Ltd: p.97; GeoScience Features Picture Library: p.98 (inset);
Zefa: pp.98-99; Topham Picture Source: p.100; Rex Features: p.101
(top); Science Photo Library: p.101 (bottom); Survival Anglia Photo
Library: pp.102-103; The Hutchinson Library: p.103 (inset);
The Meteorological Office/Colin Crane: p.104; Science
Photo Library: p.108; Topham Picture Source: p.109 (top);
The Telegraph Colour Library: p.109 (bottom)
Illustration credits: Francis Mosley: pp.90, 91, 93, 94, 97, 99, 100, 104,
105, 106, 107, 108; Linden Artists/Francis Phillipps: pp.110-114

Printed in Malaysia by Times Publishing Group

CONTENTS

Words marked in **bold** are explained in the glossary

Volcanoes

WHAT IS A VOLCANO?

Volcanoes are openings in the surface of the Earth from which gas and hot molten, or liquid, rock escape and cover the surrounding land. Some volcanoes are simply long cracks in the ground. Others look like cone-shaped mountains with a hole in the top. The hole is called a **vent**.

While the molten rock is inside the Earth, it is known as **magma**. But when it escapes on to the Earth's surface, it is called **lava**. As lava flows, it cools and hardens. The hardened lava, as well as ash and cinders from the volcano, pile up around the vent to create the **cone**.

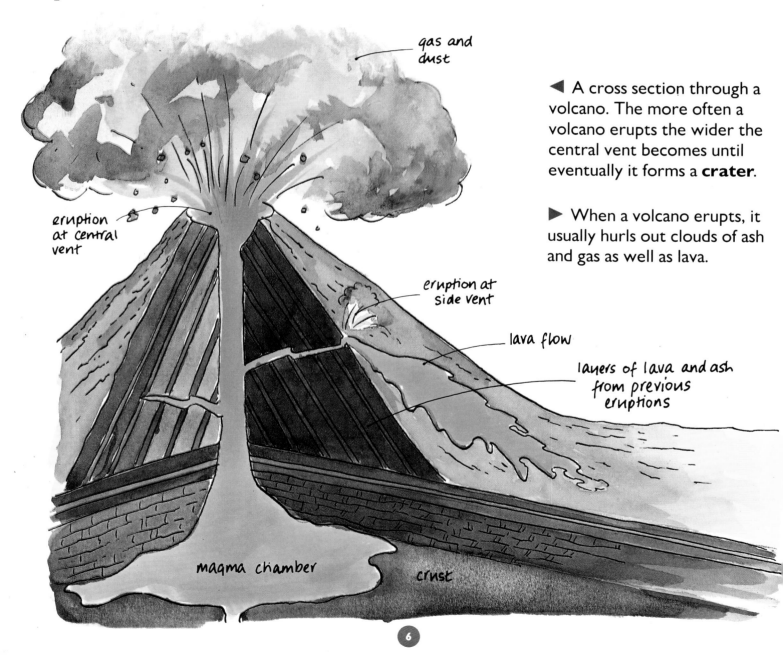

gas and dust

eruption at central vent

◀ A cross section through a volcano. The more often a volcano erupts the wider the central vent becomes until eventually it forms a **crater**.

▶ When a volcano erupts, it usually hurls out clouds of ash and gas as well as lava.

eruption at side vent

lava flow

layers of lava and ash from previous eruptions

magma chamber

crust

crust

mantle

outer
core

inner
core

The inside of the Earth is divided into different layers. The thin surface layer, called the **crust**, is made up of slabs, or plates, of rock. These float on a layer of hot, liquid rock called the **mantle**. Next comes the outer **core**, which is made up of hot, liquid metals, and the inner core, which is solid iron.

VOLCANIC ERUPTIONS

A volcanic eruption is a spectacular and often terrifying sight. Red-hot lava may burst out of the volcano with a deafening roar creating beautiful but deadly fire fountains of glowing lava which shoot hundreds of metres into the air. If the lava is very runny it may spill out of openings in the side of the volcano as well as from the central vent and pour down the mountainside in fiery rivers. These lava streams can travel great distances and will burn, bury or flatten anything in their path.

▶ This lava flow from Mauna Loa, one of Hawaii's many volcanoes, is very runny. It will travel a long way before it cools and hardens.

▼ Fire fountains erupt from twin cones on Mount Etna on the island of Sicily. Red-hot lava flows from the mountain's base.

DID YOU KNOW?

● Stromboli, a volcano off the coast of Italy, erupts once every 20 minutes! It's known as the lighthouse of the Mediterranean.

● On average, between 20 and 30 volcanoes erupt each year.

● Mauna Loa on Hawaii is the largest live volcano on Earth. One eruption lasted for one and a half years!

● The volcanoes on Hawaii, like the one in the diagram below, have wide, gently sloping cones. Because the runny lava from these volcanoes flows and spreads so quickly, the cones do not have the chance to build up to any great height.

THE RISING CLOUD

Sometimes the magma in a volcano is stiff and thick. The gases trapped in it cannot escape easily, so when the eruption comes it is very violent. Sometimes the magma hardens in the pipe leading up to the vent, blocking the flow until the pressure builds up to a point where the whole volcano may be blown apart in one massive explosion. The top of the volcano often collapses into its own magma chamber, forming a large circular crater called a **caldera**.

► Eruptions like these can throw out huge clouds of ash which bury the surrounding countryside and destroy animals, plants and even people.

VOLCANIC MATERIALS

Lava is either very runny, or stiff and thick. Different volcanoes produce these different lava types. But some volcanoes produce no liquid lava at all. Instead they shoot out solid pieces of rock. The tiniest pieces are known as **volcanic ash**. The largest ones are called **volcanic bombs**.

Volcanoes may also produce choking clouds of steam and poisonous gases. These can rush down the mountain at over 160 km an hour, smothering the surrounding countryside.

Volcanic dust from eruptions can be spread over a huge area. Dust particles which are carried into the sky may produce brilliant red sunsets in many parts of the world.

▲ This huge area of hardened lava is known as a lava field.

▼ This valley is covered in a thick layer of volcanic dust. As it is washed into the ground, the dust will make the soil very fertile.

▲ **Pumice**, a type of rock light enough to float in water, may be formed when lava cools very quickly. The tiny bubbles are created by gases escaping from the lava as it cools.

▲ As lava cools, it hardens and forms unusual patterns on the ground. Runny lava produces this wrinkled, rope-like surface known as **pahoehoe** (pronounced pa-hoh-ee-hoh-ee).

WHERE VOLCANOES ARE FOUND

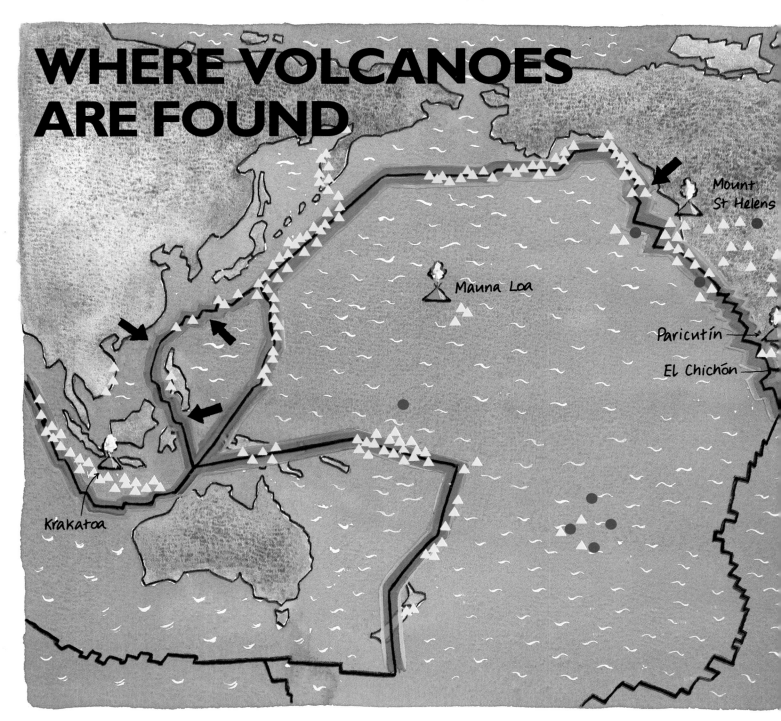

Mount St Helens

Mauna Loa

Paricutín

El Chichón

Krakatoa

The Earth's crust is not solid. It is made up of huge, moving pieces of rock called **plates**, each about 100 km thick. These plates float on the hot liquid rock of the mantle.

Volcanoes usually form where two plates collide and one is forced to slide beneath the other – as, for example, in the so-called **Ring of Fire** around the

▲ This map shows the Earth's plates and also the location of many live volcanoes.

Pacific Ocean. But other volcanoes, such as those in Hawaii, are not caused by plate movement. Instead they form **hotspots**, areas of fierce heat in the mantle which cause magma to bubble up towards the surface.

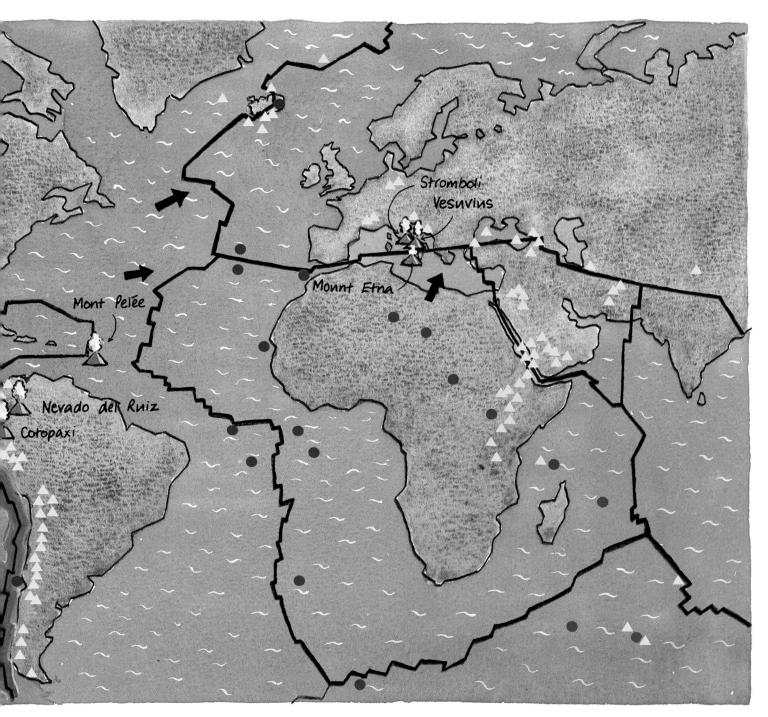

Stromboli
Vesuvius

Mont Pelée

Mount Etna

Nevado del Ruiz
Cotopaxi

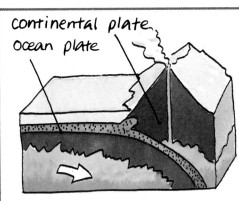

continental plate
ocean plate

When a moving ocean plate collides with a continental plate, it is forced down under the land mass. As it slides, it starts to melt. This creates magma which rises slowly up through the continental plate to create volcanoes.

Key to map

 Live volcanoes

● Hotspots

➡ Direction of plate movement

⌐⌐ Plate edges

 Ring of Fire

VOLCANIC ISLANDS

Some of the Earth's most spectacular scenery lies beneath the sea. As well as deep trenches and sweeping valleys, there are great mountains which rise from the ocean floor. Many of these mountains are volcanoes. When an underwater volcano erupts, the lava hardens into rock as it meets the water. Repeated eruptions may cause the volcano to build up to such a great height that its tip emerges from the sea.

▼ White Island lies off the eastern coast of New Zealand's North Island, in the so-called Bay of Plenty. There are a number of similar volcanic islands scattered around New Zealand's coastline.

As an underwater volcano explodes, it throws out lava which cools and hardens. A cone-shaped mountain forms around the vent.

The volcano grows with each eruption until its tip is just below sea level. Gas and lava from the next eruption rise above the waves and the tip of the volcano breaks the surface.

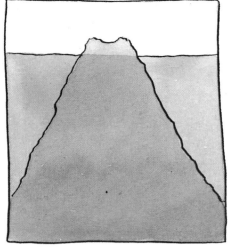

The tip of the volcano now lies above sea level. A volcanic island has been born.

In 1963, the crew of a fishing boat off the coast of Iceland saw a column of smoke in the distance. As they sailed closer, billowing clouds of ash and steam began to rise above the waves. The fishermen were witnessing the birth of a volcanic island! As the tip of the new island broke the surface of the water, red-hot lava began to pour from dozens of vents in its cone. That night, the island was 11 m high. Four days later, it was as high as two houses, and 650 m long.

The island was named Surtsey. Scientists came from all over the world to see this exciting event, and to study the growth of animal and plant life. Surtsey kept on growing and changing for almost four years. By 1967, after the last eruption of lava, the island covered more than 2.6 km^2.

▼ Clouds of ash and steam pour from one of the lava vents on Iceland's new volcanic island of Surtsey.

HOT SPRINGS AND GEYSERS

The red-hot magma in the Earth's mantle can create **hot springs** and **geysers**. These are formed where rainwater seeps down into rock above the magma chamber and is then heated. The warm water can bubble back to the surface in the form of a hot spring, or shoot upwards as a jet of steam called a geyser.

Some geysers erupt at regular intervals. A geyser's fountain of steam rises and falls because once the steam has escaped, the geyser pipe refills with water and the process starts all over again.

If the warm water mixes with the soil and chemicals underground, hot mud pools are produced. These boil and bubble on the Earth's surface.

▲ Yellowstone Park in Wyoming, USA, has over 2,500 active geysers and hot springs.

◄ Some people believe that bathing in mud pools can cure certain illnesses.

MAKE A VOLCANO

You will need:
- A small, empty, clean bottle such as an ink bottle or perfume bottle
- A piece of card
- A pin
- A small glass
- Food colouring
- Water

1 Using the pin, make a small hole in the centre of the card.

2 Half-fill the glass with cold water.

3 Put four or five drops of food colouring into the bottle, then fill the bottle with hot water from the tap.

4 Place the card over the top of the glass and hold it in place. Quickly turn the glass over, still holding the card, and place the card and glass on top of the bottle. The water won't fall out as long as you hold the card firmly over the top of the glass. But if you do spill the water, just fill the glass and start again!

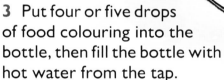

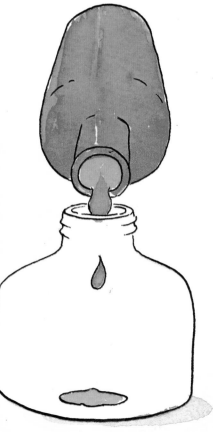

5 Still holding the card, press down gently on the glass. Puffs of colour will rise through the pin-hole into the glass. (Warm water is lighter than cold water, so the warm water rises!)

LIVING NEAR A VOLCANO

Throughout history people have lived near volcanoes. This can be dangerous, as in 1883 when the volcanic island of Krakatoa in Indonesia exploded. The explosion, which was heard 4,800 km away, killed 36,000 people on or near the island.

Even when the eruption is not so violent, clouds of poisonous gas can kill people and wildlife over a wide area. This happened in 1986 in West Africa, when carbon dioxide gas poured out from a lake in the crater of a volcano. Lava flows can engulf whole towns. In 1973, the town of Vestmannajyer on the island of Heimaey, Iceland, was buried under tonnes of red-hot lava from an eruption of Eldjfell volcano.

However, there are some advantages to living near a volcano. Volcanic soil is very rich in chemicals which are needed by plants, so it is good for growing vines and food crops such as rice and potatoes. Many important minerals like copper and nickel are mined from volcanic rocks.

▲ A flow of volcanic mud swept through the town of Armero in Colombia, South America, in 1986, killing many people.

▼ The town of Vestmannajyer, Iceland, was overwhelmed by lava in 1973. The islanders sprayed the lava with sea water for five months to try to halt its flow.

▶ Mineral-rich volcanic soil is perfect for growing rice. Farmers terrace the steep hillsides to prevent the valuable soil being washed away by rain.

◀ These Japanese macaques, or 'snow monkeys', live in the often freezing temperatures and snowy conditions of the high forests of Japan. They keep warm by bathing in hot springs.

TYPES OF VOLCANO

Volcanoes are now classified as being live or dead. A live volcano is one which may erupt in the future. A dead volcano is one which may not erupt in the future. While a live volcano is erupting, it is referred to as **active.** When it is not erupting it is said to be **dormant**.

After an eruption a live volcano may go quiet for a long period. It becomes just like any other mountain. Snow may settle on its summit and there are no signs of life. A live volcano can remain dormant like this for many years. However, deep below the surface, the huge pressure of the magma may build up, and further eruptions may occur many years later.

When a volcano is truly dead, the magma below it sinks back into the depths of the Earth. Eventually the weather wears away the cone until only the **volcanic plug** of solidified lava is left.

▲ Crater Lake, USA. Sometimes the cone of a live volcano collapses inwards forming a huge round crater called a caldera. The caldera can fill with water forming a circular lake. The island seen here is a new volcanic cone.

▲ Eroded volcanic craters on the Galapagos Islands in the Pacific Ocean provide important wildlife habitats for creatures such as this land iguana.

▼ Mount Fuji, the highest mountain in Japan, last erupted in 1707.

▲ The chapel of St Michel d'Aguiche in the French town of Le Puy sits on top of an 80m pillar of rock which was once the central pipe of a volcano.

SCIENCE AT WORK

For years scientists have been trying to find ways of predicting when volcanoes are going to erupt, so that people living in the area have time to reach safety.

Before an eruption, there are often small underground earthquakes, caused by the magma splitting rocks apart as it rises to the surface. An instrument called a **seisometer** helps scientists pinpoint the exact position of the rising magma. In Hawaii, this technique has been so successful that the time and place of eruptions has been forecast accurately.

In the scientific observatory near Mount Etna, scientists can actually hear the magma pouring through pipes within the volcano. As it does so,

▼ Scientists who study volcanoes are called vulcanologists. When they are observing an erupting volcano, they have to wear special heat-resistant suits.

it makes a sort of 'singing' sound. By listening to this 'singing', scientists can follow the magma's movements and try to predict which of the volcano's vents it might break through during the next eruption.

When magma pushes up from below, the sides of a volcano may begin to swell. This causes the ground to tilt. The tilt can be measured using an instrument called a **tiltmeter**, and again this helps scientists to tell where an eruption is going to occur.

Studying volcanic ash can reveal a lot about previous eruptions. Scientists can work out how big they were, how long they lasted, and what areas they affected. It is even possible to calculate the gap between eruptions, and therefore when the next eruption might occur.

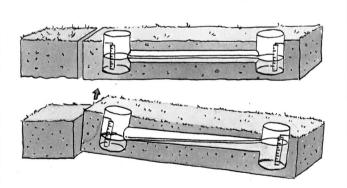

The tiltmeter consists of two containers of liquid, set several metres apart and joined by a tube. If the ground tilts, liquid runs from one container to the other. The change in the levels of the liquid indicates the amount of tilt.

DID YOU KNOW?

● Scientists now believe that the gas and ash from volcanic eruptions can cause huge changes to the weather by blocking the sun's rays and reducing the world's temperature. In 1816, the eruption of Tambora near Java caused winter weather in the middle of summer in America and Europe. The Americans nicknamed that year 'Eighteen hundred and froze to death'.

● Scientists have developed ways of using the heat inside the Earth's volcanic areas. Most of the houses in Reykjavik, the capital of Iceland, for example, are heated by hot water which is piped from underground heat sources. And power stations in New Zealand, Italy, America, Japan, Mexico and Chile use steam from underground to help generate electricity. Energy from these hot zones below the surface of the Earth is known as **geothermal energy**.

BIRTH OF A VOLCANO

Dionisio Pulido awoke with a start. Dawn was breaking, and sunlight was streaming through the tiny window above his bed. Dionisio lay for a moment, watching and listening, trying to work out what had interrupted his sleep. Suddenly the walls of his hut began to tremble. The floor creaked and groaned as the old wooden planks were disturbed. Even his bed seemed to be moving. Dionisio murmured a silent prayer, asking God to protect him, his family and all the villagers from the strangely angry earth.

It was February 1943. For fifteen days now, the Mexican village of Paricutin where Dionisio lived had been experiencing small earthquakes. Each day the tremors grew a little stronger and more frequent. In one day alone there had been over 500! The villagers were very frightened.

As soon as the tremors stopped, Dionisio jumped out of bed. He was a farmer with fields close to the village. He planned to plough his cornfield today, ready for the new seed. He must try to put the earthquakes out of his mind. He had work to do!

Dionisio hitched his oxen to the plough and set to work. It was a bitterly cold day, but Dionisio noticed that the soil beneath his feet felt quite warm. At first this puzzled him, but he soon forgot about it as the hard work of ploughing began to make him feel tired and sore.

In one corner of the field there was an outcrop of rock with a small hollow in it. This hollow had been there for as long as Dionisio could remember, and the village children often played in it.

As Dionisio neared that corner of the field, in the late afternoon, he noticed a crack in the ground by the rock. It was about 25 metres long, and went straight through the hollow.

Dionisio walked forwards to look at the crack more carefully. As he did so, he heard a loud, rumbling sound like thunder which seemed to come from beneath his feet. Smoke began to rise from the hollow and the trees at the edge of the field began to sway. Suddenly, the ground around the rock split wide open and bulged up. Dionisio was terrified. As he turned to run, smoke began to pour out of the crack, followed by sparks which set the trees on fire. The smell of sulphur filled the air. Dionisio ran as if the devil were after him! He had no idea that what he was seeing was the birth of a volcano.

As Dionisio raced into the village, shouting at the top of his voice, the villagers gathered quickly to find out

what had happened. Dionisio pointed to his field. In the distance, they could now see red-hot rock emerging from a hole at the end of the crack. This hole grew bigger and bigger as they watched.

Some of the villagers stayed up all night, fearful yet fascinated at the same time. Others prayed in the church. At 8 o'clock the following morning, Dionisio went back to his cornfield. He found that a 10 metre high cone had grown overnight – and it was still growing! By midday the cone was about 45 metres high, and by nightfall, red-hot lava was beginning to pour slowly from its base. The next morning, Dionisio had no field left.

That day, those villagers who had not already fled decided it was time to escape. And just in time! During the next week, the volcano grew to a height of 140 metres. Fragments of magma were thrown almost a kilometre into the air. The noise of the explosions could be heard in Mexico City, 816 kilometres away.

As the villagers left, scientists began to arrive from all over the world to watch and study this new volcano. The village of Paricutin, and the nearby village of San Juan Parangaricutiro were both destroyed. Vast quantities of volcanic ash covered the countryside for 12 kilometres around. Only the top of the church in San Juan Parangaricutiro could be seen above the lava. Cattle grew thin and died from lack of grazing. Water was scarce because the rivers were clogged with ash and rocks. Birds were overcome by poisonous gases and dropped dead from the sky.

The volcano kept on erupting and growing until 1952. Then 9 years and 52 days after its dramatic birth it grew calm quite suddenly. When Dionisio Pulido brought his grandchildren to visit the spot where he had once lived and worked, the huge cone of volcanic debris stood 410 metres above his cornfield. What a story he had to tell them!

TRUE OR FALSE?

Which of these facts are true and which ones are false?
If you have read this book carefully, you will know the answers.

1 All volcanoes are cone-shaped mountains.

2 The Ring of Fire is a volcano on Hawaii.

3 Scientists who study volcanoes are called vulcanologists.

4 The centre of the Earth is known as the crust.

5 Lava is the name given to magma when it escapes on to the Earth's surface.

6 Rice and other food crops grow well in volcanic soil.

7 Volcanic dust can cause red sunsets.

8 Stromboli is the largest live volcano on Earth.

9 A caldera is another name for a magma chamber.

10 The Earth's crust is made up of huge pieces of rock called plates.

11 As runny lava cools and hardens, it produces a wrinkled surface known as pahoehoe.

12 Hotspots are areas on the Earth's surface where volcanoes always form.

13 Volcanic bombs are large pieces of rock which are sometimes thrown out during a volcanic eruption.

Icebergs

WHAT ARE ICEBERGS?

Icebergs are floating masses of frozen fresh water. They are found in the world's cold seas near the North and South Poles. But where do they come from and how are they made?

Some of the land around the North and South Poles is mountainous. Near the tops of the mountains are huge snowfields where the snow gradually turns to ice. After months, or even years, the ice becomes so heavy that it starts to move slowly downhill. These 'ice rivers' are called **glaciers**. When a glacier finally reaches the sea, huge pieces of ice may break off and form floating icebergs.

Much of the Arctic, the area around the North Pole, is covered by a thick layer of ice called an **ice sheet**. Long tongues of ice extend into the sea from the edge of this ice sheet. Cracks in the ice, caused by the warmer spring weather as well as by the action of the waves, result in chunks of ice breaking off from the tongues. These too become icebergs.

An even thicker sheet of ice called the **Polar icecap** covers much of Antarctica, the area around the South Pole. Here, enormous **tabular icebergs**, so-called because of their flat, table-like tops, break off and drift out to sea.

► Icebergs drifting in the cold Arctic Ocean.

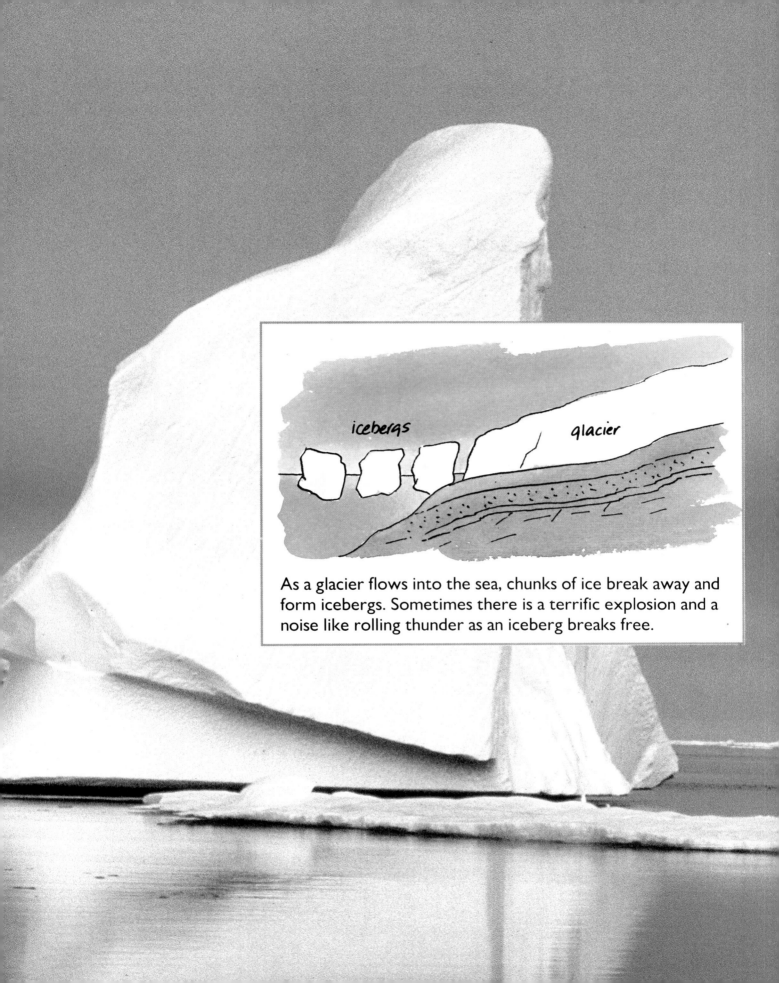

icebergs

glacier

As a glacier flows into the sea, chunks of ice break away and form icebergs. Sometimes there is a terrific explosion and a noise like rolling thunder as an iceberg breaks free.

FLOATING ICE

When most things freeze, they become smaller. However, when water freezes, it expands. This means any volume of ice will always be lighter than the equal volume of liquid water. This simple fact is what makes icebergs float.

When water freezes, it forms beautiful ice crystals. The ice itself can be clear, like huge blocks of glass. However, icebergs usually look white because of tiny gas bubbles trapped in the ice or because they are covered with snow.

► Look at this piece of floating ice. Can you see how much of it is hidden beneath the water?

Icebergs don't float all that well. Between six-sevenths and nine-tenths of any iceberg will always be under water. The fact that so much of an iceberg is out of sight, under the sea, is what makes it such a danger to ships.

▲ Around the North and South Poles, ice forms on the sea in winter.

▼ Tiny flower-like crystals form on the sea ice.

MAKE AN ICEBERG

You can see for yourself how ice floats by filling a glass with water and dropping in two ice cubes. When you have finished watching your icebergs, you can drink your experiment!

ICEBERG SHAPES AND SIZES

Icebergs come in all shapes and sizes. The largest icebergs can rise more than 120 m above the sea, and the tabular bergs may be many kilometres long. Some icebergs look like mountains. Others have been compared to towers, church spires, pyramids, cathedrals and palaces. Many are moulded into unusual and fascinating shapes by the action of the wind and the waves. The process of melting causes an iceberg to change shape too.

DID YOU KNOW?

● The largest iceberg ever recorded was 335 km long and 97 km wide, a total of 31,000 km^2 – larger than Belgium!

● The tallest iceberg ever recorded was 167 m high – just over half the height of the Eiffel Tower in Paris!

ICE ON THE MOVE

Icebergs are formed in the two coldest regions of the world, the Arctic and the Antarctic.

Arctic icebergs come mainly from Greenland. This huge island is almost entirely covered by an ice sheet. The icebergs break off, float down the coast and out into the Atlantic Ocean. In May, June and July they drift down the eastern coast of North America. Ocean liners travelling between Europe and New York always follow a more southerly route during these early summer months, to avoid the drifting bergs.

Ships and aeroplanes report the position of icebergs to the International Ice Patrol, which keeps track of the movement of icebergs in the Atlantic and estimates the routes they might take.

▼ A group of Antarctic icebergs floating free in open water during the summer season. Icebergs can travel up to 25 km per day.

▲ A tabular berg drifting away from an ice shelf into warmer waters.

The weather in the Antarctic is much colder and stormier than in the Arctic, and southern icebergs tend to be much bigger than northern ones. Most are tabular bergs which break off from the massive **ice shelves** that make up 30 per cent of Antarctica's coastline.

It can take years for an iceberg to melt. Although the wind and sun melt its surface as it drifts along on the ocean currents, the bottom section, which is under water, melts much more slowly. But when an iceberg reaches warmer waters, the melting process speeds up and the berg begins to break up into hundreds of small pieces. Eventually these melt completely and disappear.

DID YOU KNOW?

An Arctic iceberg has reached as far south as the island of Bermuda, a journey of 4,000 km, and an Antarctic iceberg has reached almost as far north as Rio de Janeiro, a journey of 5,500 km.

LIVING ON ICEBERGS

The icy seas and land masses of the Arctic and the Antarctic may seem unlikely places for animals to live, but they are home to certain types of penguins, seals and whales as well as to walruses and polar bears. Each of these animals is specially adapted for living there. A penguin, for example, has short, tightly packed feathers which form a waterproof covering over its body as well as a layer of fat under its skin to keep it warm in the cold water. Some seals have a layer of fat too. Others have thick fur to protect them against the cold.

Walruses

Walruses are members of the seal family and are found in the Arctic, near the North Pole. They live in groups called colonies, and often drift along lying on icebergs. An adult male can reach 3.7m in length and can weigh up to 1,400 kg.

The walrus spends much of its time in the water, digging for food on the sea bed with its long tusks. Clams, mussels and shrimps are its favourite meal. It crushes the shells in its mouth then spits them out, swallowing only the soft, fleshy parts of the fish. The moustache of long stiff whiskers on the walrus's face helps guide the food into its mouth.

▲ A walrus's tusks are long, upper teeth. Sometimes a walrus digs its tusks into the ice as support while it hauls itself out of the water.

▶ A humpback whale is a baleen whale. It eats krill and grows up to 15m long.

Whales

All whales live in the sea. Most are toothed whales, which feed on fish and animals such as seals. They have short, cone-shaped teeth. But others are **baleen** whales, which feed on tiny shrimp-like creatures called **krill**. Instead of teeth, a baleen whale has a series of bony plates hanging from the roof of its mouth. These act like a sieve and help the whale catch the tiny krill.

Toothed whales are constantly on the move round the world's oceans, following the shoals of fish they feed on. Baleen whales, on the other hand, make regular journeys between summer feeding grounds and winter breeding areas.

▲ Polar bears and walruses live only in the Arctic, penguins only in the Antarctic. Seals are found in both places and whales swim in most of the world's seas.

Polar bears

The polar bear is one of the largest and most ferocious land-living carnivores (meat-eaters). Polar bears are found over an area of 12 million km^2 of Arctic ice.

In winter all polar bears head south towards Greenland in search of food. By trotting over the ice and swimming through the icy sea, they can travel up to 40 km in a day.

They mainly eat seals, although they have learned to scavenge from rubbish dumps and even houses in the towns of northern Canada.

Polar bears are superbly adapted for the cold. Their bodies are covered with a layer of fat called **blubber** and thick fur.

Pregnant female polar bears dig large dens in snowdrifts at the start of winter. The tunnel to the outside always slopes downwards, trapping the warm air in the den. In December the cubs are born. They are blind and completely helpless. They feed off their mother's rich milk. In March, they go out on the ice for the first time.

Penguins

Adelie penguins are one of the seven species of penguin which live in the Antarctic region. They spend most of each year at sea, but return to land to lay their eggs and raise their chicks. Once a year, too, they come ashore to **moult**. Their old feathers fall out and are replaced by new ones growing underneath.

Penguins cannot fly, but their paddle-shaped wings, short legs and webbed feet are perfectly designed for life in the water. Moving on land is more difficult. They must either waddle slowly or fall forwards on their chests and toboggan across the ice.

DID YOU KNOW?

⬤ At the end of summer, each female Emperor penguin lays one egg, then returns to the ocean. The male keeps the egg warm all winter in a fold of skin on top of his feet. He eats nothing and by the time the female returns he has lost 40 per cent of his body weight.

◀ These Adelie penguins are diving into the water in search of fish. They have special spikes inside their mouths to help them hold on to their slippery prey. They can store the food inside their bodies, in special pouches called crops.

▼ A baby seal is called a pup. It is left to survive on its own when it is about six weeks old.

▲ Three harbour seals resting on Arctic ice. Seals cannot remain beneath the surface continuously for more than 20 minutes.

Seals

Like penguins, seals are ideally suited for living in the water. Their smooth, streamlined bodies, **flippers** and short, strong tails make them excellent swimmers. On land they move slowly, wriggling and sliding across the ice.

Seals spend most of their lives at sea, but come ashore to mate and for the females to give birth to their young.

At one time, seals were killed for their fur which was used to make coats, hats and boots. Now many people do not like wearing clothes made of animal fur, and the killing of seals in large numbers is forbidden.

ICEBREAKERS

An icebreaker is a ship which has been designed to travel through ice-covered waters. It has a specially shaped **bow** and a reinforced **hull**. Icebreakers move slowly but steadily, pushing their bows up on top of the ice until the weight of the ship causes the ice to collapse. The largest icebreakers are designed to break ice that is 2.4 m thick. But by reversing and then ramming the ice, some can actually break through ice more than 7 m thick!

Icebreakers are used to rescue ships trapped in ice, conduct scientific research and escort supply ships. The Soviet Union uses some of the world's largest icebreakers to clear ice from its shipping lanes in the Arctic.

▲ A pause in the journey while some research is carried out on the ice.

CROSSING THE ICE

In the past, explorers crossed the ice on foot or used sledges pulled by **huskies**. Modern explorers can choose from many different means of transport.

The fastest way of travelling across the ice is by air. Quite large planes are fitted with skis so they can land on the snow. Helicopters can land on single icebergs. Tractors called snowcats, with caterpillar tracks, carry heavy loads across the ice. Lightweight snow scooters, known as skidoos, skim quickly over the surface.

▼ Huskies have pulled sledges across the ice for hundreds of years.

▲ Tents must be securely pitched, as strong winds and blizzards can occur quite suddenly.

THE TITANIC

On the night of the 14th of April 1912, the passenger liner RMS *Titanic* was steaming through the North Atlantic. She was the biggest ship ever built and this was her first voyage. The 2,227 passengers and crew were enjoying themselves, secure in the knowledge that the ship was unsinkable.

Just before midnight, some of the passengers felt a slight jolt and wondered what it was. They did not know that the great liner had hit an iceberg, nor did they realise that within two hours the *Titanic* would sink to the bottom of the ocean.

The 'unsinkable' ship only had enough lifeboats for half the people on board. In fact only 705 were actually rescued. The remaining passengers and crew were either carried to the bottom of the sea as the huge liner made its final plunge, or froze to death in the icy water.

▼ The end of the *Titanic*.

WORKING ON THE ICE

A lot of people work on the ice. The Arctic, for example, is an important oil-producing area. Oil rigs drill for oil which is then pumped southwards along a pipeline over 1,200 km long.

There are also several scientific stations in the polar regions. Scientists study the animals and other wildlife. They have found that many animals are in danger of extinction because of over-fishing and **pollution**.

Chemicals used in aerosol sprays have damaged the Antarctic ozone layer which protects us from the sun's dangerous ultraviolet radiation. A similar hole has now been found over the Arctic.

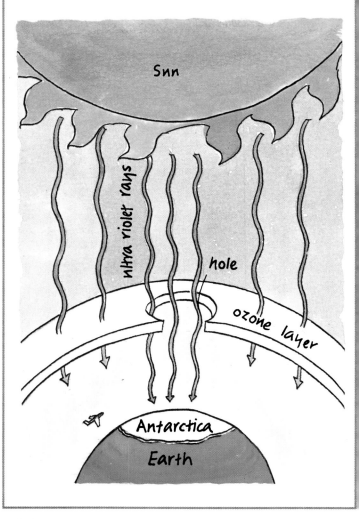

◀ A scientist explores the underwater world below the Antarctic ice. Biologists are fascinated by the variety of life forms which exist in these icy waters.

▶ The Faraday Scientific Station on the west coast of the Antarctic Peninsula. It is a laboratory for studying the atmosphere.

Scientists who study the weather have discovered that Earth's atmosphere is starting to warm up as a result of the **greenhouse effect**. They have also found evidence of serious pollution. One of their most recent discoveries is that a huge hole has appeared in the **ozone layer** of the atmosphere over Antarctica. This will lead to more **ultraviolet radiation** from the sun reaching the Earth. These ultraviolet rays will cause an increase in skin cancer. Reports of the ozone hole have alarmed people all over the world. But it may be too late to repair the damage.

▲ In 1968, oil was discovered in Prudhoe Bay, which lies in Alaska's Arctic Coastal Plain. Oil is now Alaska's most valuable mineral product.

THE STORY OF THREE WHALES

On the morning of the 7th of October 1988, Roy Ashmaogak left his home in the small town of Barrow, in the north-west of Alaska, to hunt for seals. The weather was bitterly cold. Winter had come early, and the sea around Barrow had already frozen over. But Roy had lived in Barrow all his life, so he was used to the freezing temperatures and to being surrounded by ice and snow for months on end. He had hunted seals in conditions like these many times.

But this was to be no ordinary day. As Roy tramped across the ice, something caught his eye. As he moved closer, he saw an extraordinary sight. Three California grey whales were pushing

their great heads through a crack in the ice! They seemed anxious and frightened. Roy realised at once that the whales were trapped. There was ice everywhere. The whales' noses were scraped and bruised from trying to force a way through to the open sea.

Roy guessed that the three whales must have been left behind when the rest of their herd began the long swim south from their summer feeding grounds in the Arctic Ocean to their winter breeding grounds in the warm waters of California. Surprised by the sudden, early arrival of winter they seemed to have lost their sense of direction. Instead of heading for open water, they had swum into a shallow bay where the water had quickly frozen over and formed a wall of ice at the bay's mouth. There was no way out.

Whales need to come up to the surface about every four minutes, to breathe. Roy knew that something had to be done soon to help the whales. They had managed to make one small breathing hole, but the ice was thick and they were too weak to create any more. Roy raced back to Barrow to look for help.

Everyone listened to Roy's story, but at first nothing was done. Many people felt that, sad though it was, the whales should be left to die. But others began to feel differently. A woman called Cindi Lowry began to try to interest people in the idea of saving the whales. Soon the story of the whales appeared in local newspapers and on television. The Inuit people of Barrow trooped out on to the ice with chainsaws and pickaxes to try to cut more breathing holes for the whales and guide them through to open water.

Before long, people all round the world had heard about the three whales. Scientists and others who wanted to help began to flock to Barrow to see what could be done. Even Ronald Reagan, the president of the United States of America at the time, offered his help.

But was it too late? By now, the Inuit had worked for fourteen days and nights to cut a line of breathing holes in the ice, leading towards the sea. But the holes kept freezing over and, in any case, the whales seemed too frightened to follow the trail. To make matters worse, the youngest whale, nicknamed Bone, was ill. It was wheezing with pneumonia and trying to rest its battered head on the ice shelf. Sadly, on Friday 21st of October, it died.

The two older whales, nicknamed Crossbeak and Bonnet, were tiring. Something had to be done quickly if they were to escape from their ice prison. An enormous ice barge, which looked like a gigantic bulldozer, tried to smash a path through the ice, but it got stuck. Then a sky-crane helicopter hammered the ice with a concrete weight. It punched a line of holes from the whales to the ice wall at the mouth of the bay, but Crossbeak and Bonnet still would not move. It seemed that they too would die. The rescuers were at their wits' end. They were beginning to think they might have to try to airlift the whales to safety in a huge net slung from a helicopter! But they were worried about this idea. It had never been tried before and a California grey whale, although not the largest type of whale by any means, still weighs about 30,000 kilograms!

Then, on the twentieth day, Wednesday the 26th of October, just as everyone had almost given up hope, a Russian icebreaker roared to the rescue. All day and all night the huge ship charged at the ice, smashing it into tiny pieces. By the morning of the following day, part of the ice wall at the bay's mouth had been destroyed and a clear, narrow channel led from the whales to the open sea. A great cheer went up from the captain and his crew and from all the others who had been involved in the rescue. Three weeks after they had first been spotted, the whales were free!

The icebreaker turned and headed homewards. The whales followed close behind. At last they were on their way to join the rest of the herd on the long journey south.

TRUE OR FALSE?

Which of these facts are true and which ones are false?
If you have read this book carefully, you will know the answers.

1 A glacier is a type of iceberg.

2 Antarctic icebergs tend to be bigger than those found in the Arctic.

3 Between one-seventh and one-tenth of an iceberg is under water.

4 Walruses are found in the Arctic.

5 Tiny gas bubbles trapped in the ice cause an iceberg to look white.

6 The International Ice Patrol monitors the movement of icebergs in Antarctica.

7 Killer whales are baleen whales.

8 Female polar bears give birth to their cubs in snow dens which they dig at the start of winter.

9 The largest iceberg ever recorded was the same size as Belgium.

10 Icebergs are often moulded into unusual shapes by the action of the wind and the waves.

11 There are two main groups of icebergs – tabular and rounded.

12 An icebreaker is a type of sledge used for travelling across the ice.

13 Penguins cannot fly.

Answers: 1 False; 2 True; 3 False; 4 True; 5 True; 6 False; 7 False; 8 True; 9 False; 10 True; 11 False; 12 False; 13 True.

Jungles

WHAT IS A JUNGLE?

A jungle is an area of densely packed trees and plants. The word is usually used to describe tropical rainforests. These forests lie near the Equator, the imaginary line around the centre of the Earth. Rain falls almost every day, and the temperature varies very little between the hottest and the coldest month. Tropical rainforests are packed with all kinds of vegetation, from trees and creepers to shrubs and brightly coloured flowers. About half the world's **species** of plants and animals are found in tropical rainforests.

▶ Tropical rainforest in Australia.

◀ The layers of vegetation in a tropical rainforest.
Emergent layer Some trees grow as tall as 61 m.
Canopy layer The trees in this layer grow from 30 to 46 m tall. Their tops or crowns form a roof of leaves over the forest.
Understory or 'middle' layer The shorter trees that grow beneath the canopy form this layer. They reach a height of about 20 m.
Shrub layer This layer consists of short, woody plants which have more than one stem. The tall trees filter out so much sunlight that few shrubs are able to grow.
Forest floor Very little sunlight reaches the forest floor. A thick covering of leaves, twigs and animal droppings, as well as the remains of dead animals and plants, builds up.

ALL AROUND THE WORLD

Tropical rainforests cover about seven per cent of the surface of the Earth. They occupy large areas of Central and South America, West Africa, and Asia. Smaller areas occur in Australia and in Papua New Guinea. All tropical rainforests are similar, but different animal and plant species are found in each of the different continents.

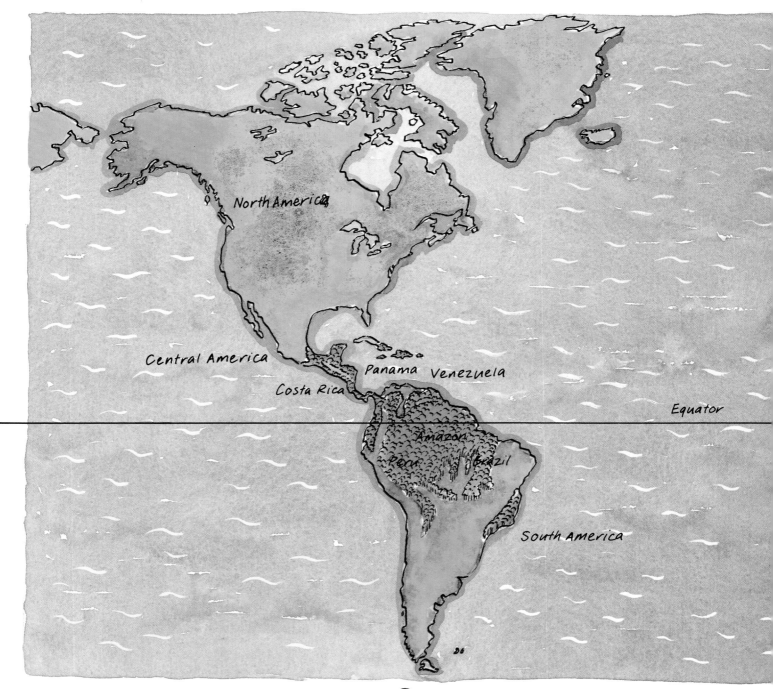

The world's tropical rainforests are in great danger. They are being cut down to provide timber and firewood, and to make room for homes, roads, farms and factories. Some areas are being cleared to allow oil and valuable **minerals** such as gold to be mined. Scientists estimate that about 17 million hectares are now being destroyed every year. The **habitats** of thousands of species of animals and plants have already vanished. The way of life of many rainforest peoples is also under threat from these changes.

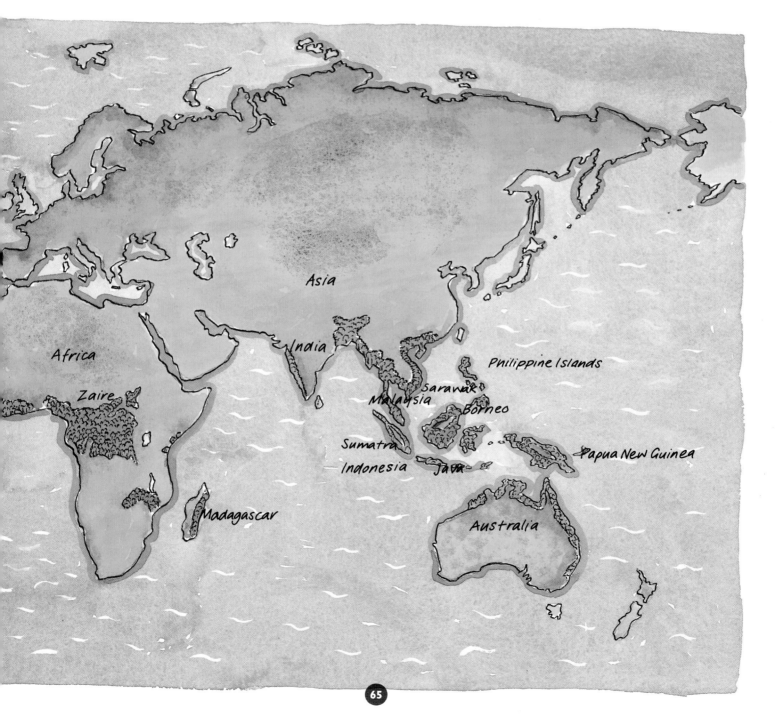

Asia

India

Africa

Philippine Islands

Zaire

Sarawak
Malaysia
Borneo

Sumatra

Papua New Guinea

Indonesia   Java

Madagascar

Australia

CREEPERS AND CLIMBERS

Trees and plants thrive in the warm, damp conditions of a tropical rainforest. There is always a tree or plant bearing fruit, and the forest is always green.

Most tropical rainforest trees are **evergreens**. They only have branches near the tops of their trunks. The leaves are dark green and tough, with pointed drip-tips to let the rainwater run off. Climbing plants called lianas loop from tree to tree like huge ropes tying the whole forest together. Plants like ferns, mosses, orchids and **bromeliads** grow on the trunks and branches of living trees.

▲ Rainforests contain many interesting plants. Some of these, such as palms and orchids, have become popular house plants.

◀ In tropical rainforests, plants known as **epiphytes** grow high on the trees, close to the sunlight. They get food and moisture from the air.

▶ The roots of some tropical rainforest trees form wide, spreading growths around the tree's base. These buttress roots help keep the tree upright.

◄ The pitcher plant feeds off insects, which are trapped in its tube-shaped leaves. A sweet smell given off by tiny glands inside the top edge of the leaves attracts insects to the plant. When an insect lands, it is trapped by the plant's bristly hairs. It then slides down into the tube.

DID YOU KNOW?

● There are more kinds of trees in a tropical rainforest than in any other area of the world. In one section of rainforest in South America, scientists counted 179 different species of trees in an area the size of a large garden.

● About 155,000 of the 250,000 known species of plants are found in tropical rainforests.

● The giant rafflesia produces the largest flowers of any known plant. Unfortunately, the flowers usually smell very unpleasant.

● A scientist at Harvard University, USA, has worked out that it would take 25,000 scientists the whole of their working lives to record all the known **flora and fauna** of the world's tropical rainforests.

ROAMING THE JUNGLE

Many of the animals in a tropical rainforest spend their lives high up in the trees, where there are always flowers, leaves, fruit and nuts to eat. They have developed ways of moving through the canopy in search of food. Some, like monkeys, are very agile and climb well. Others, such as flying **lemurs** and flying squirrels, are able to glide from tree to tree. Snakes loop themselves around the branches,

▲ Tree frogs eat insects and other small animals. Many can change colour to blend in with their surroundings. Some male tree frogs make a high-pitched squeak to attract females. In order to make this sound, the tree frog's throat swells up like a balloon.

▼ The tiger hunts alone, stalking its prey slowly and carefully. It kills its prey with a single blow of its forepaw.

while tree frogs have sticky pads on their feet to stop them falling.

Larger animals like antelope, deer and **tapirs**, as well as small rodents, roam the forest floor. They feed on roots, seeds, leaves, and fruit which has fallen to the ground. Some animals, such as gorillas, live on the ground as well as in the trees.

Although many tropical rainforest animals are plant eaters, or herbivores, others, such as jaguars and tigers, are carnivores. Carnivores hunt and kill other animals for food. The hunted

▲ Sloths, which live in the rainforests of South America, spend most of their time hanging upside-down from branches. Their claws grip the branches so securely that they can fall asleep in this position. Sloths often carry their babies on their bellies.

animals have to be on constant look-out against possible danger.

The destruction of so many areas of tropical rainforest means that many of the animals which live there are now in danger of **extinction**. Orang-utans, jaguars and gorillas are some of the rainforest animals under threat.

THE COLOURFUL CANOPY

Most tropical rainforest birds live high up in the canopy, where there is plenty of food. Hawks and eagles soar above the emergent layer, swooping down from time to time to snatch up other birds, bats, and even monkeys. Many tropical rainforest birds have very brightly coloured feathers. Although you might think this would make them easy to spot against the green of the trees, in fact the bright colours act as a kind of camouflage. The bright spots of colour can easily be mistaken for flowers or fruit.

Male bowerbirds, found in the tropical rainforests of New Guinea and Australia, build beautiful bowers or shelters in which to court their mates. The bowers are built of grass, moss, twigs and creepers, and are often decorated with brightly-coloured feathers, berries, shells and flowers.

► Tropical rainforest birds have developed different ways of feeding. Macaws use their strong beaks to crack nuts like brazil nuts with no difficulty.

◄ Hummingbirds' wings beat so fast, it is almost impossible for the human eye to detect any movement at all. The smallest member of the hummingbird family measures only 5.5 cm from the tip of its bill to the tip of its tail! Its body is about the same size as that of a large bumble-bee, and it weighs less than 2 grams. Hummingbirds have long, slender bills and long tongues which allow them to suck nectar from the centre of even the deepest tube-shaped flowers.

◄ An African grey parrot enjoying a meal. Like most other types of parrot and macaw, the African grey is able to hold its food in one foot and bite pieces off, similar to the way in which humans might eat a sandwich! The parrot keeps its balance by curling its other foot around the branch. A parrot's foot has four toes, two of which lie to the front, the other two to the rear, so it is easy for the bird to grip the branch tightly and securely.

THE TINIEST CREATURES

Scientists believe that up to 80% of all the world's insect species live only in tropical rainforests. A recent study of a one-hectare area of a rainforest in Peru found 41,000 different types of insect species living in the canopy alone. There may be between 1 million and 10 million insect species still undiscovered, so, if you spent a day in a tropical rainforest collecting insects, you would probably find one that no one else had ever seen.

Insects are fascinating creatures. Most of them smell with their **antennae**; some taste with their feet. Some have no eyes; others have five eyes or more. Many are very strong – an ant, for example, can lift an object 50 times heavier than its own body weight.

▲ This insect is a type of giant weevil. Its antennae are positioned half-way down its long nose, at the end of which is its mouth. A female weevil uses her long nose to drill a hole in which to lay her eggs.

◄ Leafcutter ants cut pieces of leaves from trees, plants and shrubs. They carry the leaves back to their nest, holding them above their heads. Inside the nest, the ants chew the leaves into a pulp which is then left to rot. The ants feed on a fungus which grows on the rotting pulp.

Insects are great survivors, too. They can live in places that are too small for other animals and they need little food. An insect's skeleton is on the outside of its body, which protects it against injury and prevents its body losing moisture. Being able to fly makes it easier to find food and escape from enemies.

◀ This crab spider can disguise itself by changing the colour of its body to match the colour of the flower blossom in which it is crawling. Scientists call spiders arachnids because they are different from insects. They have eight legs, whereas insects have only six.

▼ The bright colours of this young grasshopper suggest that it might be a poisonous insect. This stops enemies such as spiders and beetles approaching.

LIVING IN THE JUNGLE

Some tribes of people live deep in the jungle, just as their ancestors have done for generations. Many of them farm using a method called slash-and-burn cultivation. First, they chop down trees to clear a space in the forest. They burn the trees and plant seeds among the ashes. The crops grow quickly in the warm, moist ground. After a few years, the thin layer of soil

▼ Some houses, like this one in Indonesia, are built on stilts if the ground is swampy.

DID YOU KNOW?

● The Efe people, a **pygmy** tribe who live in the Ituri Forest in Zaire, build huts from saplings and leaves. The saplings are driven into the soft ground, then bent over into a dome shape. Branches are woven through the bent saplings and the whole framework is covered with leaves.

● Some people who live in the Amazon rainforest build shelters big enough to house a whole community. The shelters are the shape of wheels, with an open centre.

● The Kraho Indians of Brazil arrange their villages in the shape of a wheel. The houses are built around the edge of the wheel. Pathways lead to the centre, where the villagers hold meetings.

loses its goodness and crops no longer grow well. The people move to another area and begin again.

Rainforest people also gather fruit and plants from the forest. They hunt animals using blowpipes, poisoned darts, bows and arrows or spears.

Rainforest people build shelters which can be put up quickly, when the group arrives in a new area.

◀ Embera Indians in Panama grinding manioc plant roots. The roots contain poison so must be ground and washed before they can be eaten.

▼ A Penan man spearing fish in Sarawak, Malaysia.

CHANGING WAYS

The world's population has more than doubled in the last 40 years, and is continuing to increase at the rate of 155 people every minute. This dramatic rise causes enormous problems. People need somewhere to live and work, and they need food to eat. Huge areas of tropical rainforest have been cut down to provide areas for settlement and farming. In Brazil, for example, over a million people have been resettled in cleared

rainforest areas. But these **colonisation** schemes often fail because the soil is too poor to allow the crops to grow well.

The more people there are in the world, the more demand there is for goods such as furniture, window-frames and doors made from **tropical hardwood** such as mahogany and teak. Tropical rainforests lie mostly in the poorer countries of the world, and these countries can make a lot of money by selling timber to the world's richer countries. Other rainforest areas have been cut down to clear space for oilfields and mines.

In some tropical rainforests, loggers remove only certain trees or species of tree, rather than simply felling the whole area. But the heavy machinery used causes enormous damage. In Asia, for example, it is estimated that for every ten trees felled deliberately, another thirteen are seriously damaged.

▼ A section of the Amazon forest, cleared for settlement.

The effect of all these changes on the ways of life of many rainforest peoples has been enormous. The destruction of the forests has made it more difficult for them to survive by hunting and farming. Many of the animals and plants that they relied upon for food have died out. Huge roads have been built through the forests, and settlers, miners, **loggers**, scientists and even tourists now have access to areas which were once remote. These newcomers have brought diseases to the rainforest peoples, against which they have no resistance.

▼ The Amazon forest in South America is the largest tropical rainforest in the world. Over 10,000 km of road now runs through the forest.

WHAT USE ARE JUNGLES?

It is not hard to guess that a piece of wooden furniture may have been made from a tropical rainforest tree. However, did you know that golf balls, nail varnish, deodorant, toothpaste, chewing gum, shampoo and the glue on postage stamps are all made from or contain materials obtained from the world's tropical rainforests? Many of the foods you eat have been developed from tropical rainforest plants. When you are ill, the medicine the doctor

▼ A South American Indian collects latex to make rubber.

gives you may contain plant extracts and the hot water bottle that keeps you warm began its life as a milky juice which comes from the rubber tree.

Many of the foods we eat no longer come directly from the tropical rainforests, but are grown on large **plantations**.

Rainforest peoples have made medicines from plants for hundreds of years.It is only fairly recently though that scientists have discovered how useful tropical rainforest plants may be in producing life-saving drugs which can be used to treat people all over the world. At least 1,400 plants found in tropical rainforests are now believed to offer possible treatments against cancer.

ROTTING LEAVES

The forest floor is covered with leaves, twigs, animal droppings and the remains of dead animals. These waste materials break down and decay quickly in the moist heat, providing food for animals, insects, and plants. Try this experiment to see how leaves rot.

You will need:
- Two margarine tubs (one with a lid)
- Fresh, dry leaves
- Wet soil

1 Put some of the leaves in each tub.

2 Add wet soil to one container, and pack it round the leaves. Put the lid on this container.

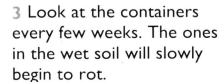

3 Look at the containers every few weeks. The ones in the wet soil will slowly begin to rot.

JUNGLES IN DANGER

If the world's tropical rainforests are to be saved from total destruction, many people believe that action must be taken now. Scientists need to find ways of supplying timber without entire forests being destroyed. They need to develop ways of putting goodness back into the soil left bare by forest clearance, and organise **reforestation** schemes.

Politicians and business people need to begin to cooperate with the native rainforest peoples, who know and understand the forests. People in rich countries need to reduce their demand for tropical hardwood and look for alternative materials.

Unless something is done quickly, all the possible benefits to the world will be lost.

The world's climate may change, too. The destruction of the tropical rainforests has added to the growing amount of carbon dioxide gas in the atmosphere. Carbon dioxide and other gases are causing an alarming change in the world's climate. This change is known as **global warming** or the **greenhouse effect**.

▶ Slash and burn cultivation used to be confined to small areas of the rainforest. Today, however, huge areas are burnt down by big companies.

◀ Every year, an area of the Amazon rainforest is flooded for six months or more. The waters can rise to a height of about 9 m. Only the tops of the tallest trees remain above water. Others are completely under water – but they go on growing! Normally, floods destroy trees, but in this area of the Amazon, when the flood waters go down, the trees have suffered no harm. This flooded forest is a unique habitat, with a huge variety of wildlife. It too is under threat.

JUNGLE RESCUE

The engine of the tiny plane coughed, spluttered and stopped. O'Reilly and Jackson looked at each other in utter horror.

"Fasten your seat belts," the pilot shouted, as the plane began to lose height. He peered anxiously through the windscreen, searching for a suitable landing spot. He could see nothing but trees. The jungle stretched like a giant green carpet as far as the eye could see.

The jungle seemed to rush up towards them. Then, with a splintering crash, the plane ploughed through the tree tops, smashing through the branches until it finally came to a halt. It hung

for a few seconds then slid, nose first, towards the ground. There was complete silence.

O'Reilly unfastened his seat-belt and looked around. The plane was wedged at an impossible angle between two giant trees. A huge branch had ripped through the thin fuselage and was sticking into the cabin. O'Reilly became aware that his fellow passenger was groaning in pain. Hauling himself across the crazily angled floor, O'Reilly examined his companion. Jackson's leg was broken.

O'Reilly spent several minutes finding the first aid kit and then two reasonably straight branches for splints. He strapped up the leg as best he could and gave Jackson some pain-killers. Then he groped his way to the cockpit. The pilot was unconscious.

O'Reilly returned to the cabin.

"The pilot's out cold and the radio's broken," he explained. "It'll be hours before anyone misses us, let alone sends out a rescue party."

Jackson nodded stiffly.

"I'll go for help," continued O'Reilly. "I spotted a clearing not far away as we were coming down. I'll be as quick as I can."

Making Jackson as comfortable as he could, O'Reilly climbed out of the plane and grabbed hold of a creeper to help him down through the trees. Within minutes, his shirt was soaked with sweat from the sticky heat. Dust and dirt stuck to his damp skin. Branches whipped him as he forced his way downwards until red scratches covered his arms and face.

When he reached the jungle floor he found to his surprise that it was quite clear. A thick layer of leaves and animal droppings covered it, but few plants barred his way. With one last glance at the plane, he set off in the direction of the clearing.

In places the trees nearly blotted out the sun, reducing the light to a green twilight. This made walking very difficult, as he could not see fallen branches, roots or ditches. He stumbled and tripped in these dark places. Swarms of insects buzzed around his face, moving only when he brushed them away with his hand, to return moments later, thicker than ever.

All around, he could hear the sounds of the jungle. Birds and monkeys chattered loudly and

branches creaked and swayed. From time to time, he caught a glimpse of larger animals between the trees, but they stayed out of his way.

O'Reilly stopped to rest when he reached the river. After hours of walking, he was exhausted.

He picked a piece of fruit off a nearby tree and ate it before going on, following the river bank.

The bank was much harder to walk on than the forest floor. A tangle of roots and slimy mud covered it. Once, O'Reilly slipped and had to grab a branch to stop himself tumbling into the water. As his foot splashed on the surface of the water, he saw the long, low form of an alligator sliding into the water. From then on, he walked more carefully.

Then, at last, he saw a flickering light through the trees. It was the campfire in a logging camp. With a last desperate burst of energy, O'Reilly staggered into the circle of firelight. The loggers started up in surprise at the sight of his scarecrow figure. O'Reilly stammered out his story.

Within minutes the logging company's helicopter had taken off. In spite of O'Reilly's accurate directions, the jungle seemed to have swallowed the wrecked plane. The helicopter criss-crossed the trees, its powerful searchlight probing the darkness below. It was over an hour before the helicopter was finally hovering over the crashed plane, while the crew winched up the injured pilot and passenger. A radio signal crackled the news to the logging camp, where O'Reilly now sat staring into the firelight, exhausted. Only when he heard that Jackson and the pilot were safe, did he at last close his eyes and fall into a deep sleep.

TRUE OR FALSE?

Which of these facts are true and which ones are false?
If you have read this book carefully, you will know the answers.

1 The Amazon forest in South America is the largest tropical rainforest in the world.

2 About a quarter of the world's species of plants and animals live in tropical rainforests.

3 All jungle animals are herbivores (plant-eaters).

4 Most tropical rainforest trees have branches only near the tops of their trunks.

5 Many tropical rainforest plants are used to cure illness and disease.

6 The climate in a tropical rainforest is cold and damp.

7 Epiphytes are a type of spider.

8 An ant can lift an object 50 times heavier than its own body weight.

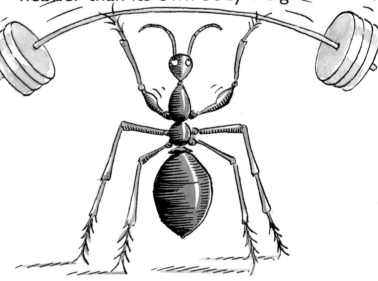

9 Many of the foods you eat have been developed from tropical rainforest plants.

10 Few tropical rainforest birds have very brightly coloured feathers.

11 The canopy forms a roof of leaves over the forest.

12 The waste materials on the forest floor provide food for animals, insects, trees and plants.

Answers: 1 True; 2 True; 3 False; 4 True; 5 True; 6 False; 7 False; 8 True; 9 True; 10 False; 11 True; 12 True.

Storms

WHAT IS A STORM?

Flashes of lightning, loud crashes of thunder, torrential rain, howling winds, driving snow! Those may be some of the things the word 'storm' conjures up in your mind. A storm is a period of very bad, often violent weather. It may include rain, hail, snow, thunder and lightning, strong winds or a mixture of these.

Weather is caused by changes in the thin blanket of air, called the **atmosphere**, which surrounds the Earth. Movements of hot and cold air as well as changes in the amount of moisture in the air mean that the atmosphere varies between being hot or cold, dry or wet, calm or windy.

Sometimes huge masses of air settle over areas of sea or land. These **air masses** become warm, cold, dry or damp, depending on the nature of the land or sea below. They bring days, even weeks of unchanging weather.

When these air masses begin to move, the problems begin! Different air masses don't mix, and if the edge or **front** of a warm air mass meets a cold air mass, or vice versa, storms are likely to occur.

▶ Dark storm clouds gathering at sunset.

clouds form

rain, hail and snow

air cools

Sun's rays heat up the Earth

▼ As the Sun's rays warm the Earth, heat and moisture are released into the atmosphere. This moisture produces clouds, rain, hail and snow.

cold air is pulled in from behind

warm, moist air rises

When cold and warm air masses meet, clouds form along each front and there are violent storms.

RAIN AND HAILSTORMS

Raindrops form when tiny water droplets in a cloud join together or when ice crystals in a cloud melt. When the raindrops become too large and heavy for the air to support them, they start to fall out of the cloud. The larger the raindrops, the faster they fall!

Hailstones are formed in much the same way as raindrops but they fall only from **cumulonimbus** clouds. The inside of a cumulonimbus cloud is very cold and the hailstones start their lives as ice particles. As these particles are thrown about inside the cloud they absorb water droplets which then freeze to them in layers, like an onion. As many as 25 layers have been found on a single hailstone!

● Most hailstones which fall are about the size of a pea, but the largest hailstone ever recorded was the size of a melon and weighed 758g. It fell in Coffeyville, Kansas, USA on September 3rd 1970.

● The driest place in the world is the desert town of Arica in Chile. It receives only about 0.76 mm of rain each year!

● The wettest place in the world is Mount Wai-'ale-'ale in Hawaii. It has rain for about 335 days of the year!

◀ Rainstorms are short periods of very heavy rain which fall over a small area. They are often accompanied by thunder and can cause **flash floods** as rivers become torrents.

▶ This cross-section of a hailstone shows the many different layers of ice.

▲ Light rays travel in straight lines but when sunlight shines through raindrops, the rays bend slightly. White light is actually made up of seven different coloured lights and each one bends in a different way. So the light splits into red, orange, yellow, green, blue, indigo and violet. This causes a rainbow to appear.

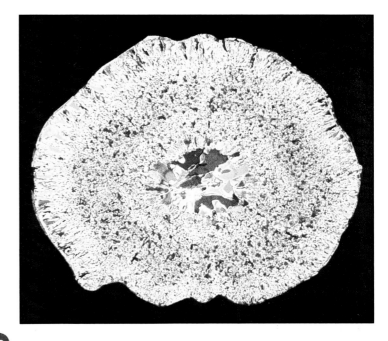

THUNDER AND LIGHTNING

Most thunderstorms happen in summer, when the air is warm and damp. As the air rises, it cools, and the moisture it contains forms huge, grey-black thunderclouds.

Fast-moving air currents inside each thundercloud cause electric charges to build up. Eventually, the electricity is released from the clouds in the form of giant sparks which we know as lightning.

When a flash of lightning leaves a cloud, it zig-zags to the ground. It then returns, racing up the same path back to the cloud. It is the bright light of this **return stroke** that we see.

Return strokes travel at about the speed of light. They discharge almost 100 million volts of electricity and heat the air in their paths to over 33,000°C The heated air expands quickly and collides with cool air, producing sound waves that we hear as thunder.

Lightning is produced when separated positive and negative electrical charges flow towards one another. As well as zig-zagging to the ground, lightning can occur within a cloud or between clouds.

► Thunderclouds often stretch several thousand metres up into the atmosphere. The fast-moving air currents inside them can hold extra-large raindrops, so thunderclouds often produce heavy rain.

▲Thunder and lightning happen at the same time, but because light travels faster than sound, we see lightning before we hear thunder.

SNOWSTORMS

When water droplets freeze on to ice particles in a cloud, the particles get bigger and become ice crystals. As these fall through the cloud, they collide with other ice crystals and become snowflakes.

Once the snowflakes are large and heavy enough, they begin to fall out of the cloud. If they fall through warmer air they melt and fall as rain. But if the air is cold they fall as snow. Snow can soon start to cause problems on the ground. A snowfall of only 10cm is enough to block roads!

A severe snowstorm is called a blizzard. These occur when snowfall is accompanied by strong winds which whip up the snow into a swirling white mist and blow it into deep piles called snowdrifts. Poor visibility and near-freezing temperatures make life very difficult in blizzard conditions.

Machines called snowploughs and snowblowers are used to clear roads

▲ Most snow crystals have six sides. Although billions of them have fallen on to the Earth, no two look exactly the same. Different weather conditions produce different shaped crystals. Needle and rod shapes form in cold air. The more complicated shapes form in warmer air.

▲ When heavy snow falls, animals often have difficulty in finding food. Farmers sometimes have to take bales of hay out to the fields.

after severe snowstorms, but even they can find it difficult to clear deep snow from remote areas. People who live in these places can be 'snowed in' for days, even weeks. Even in large cities, daily life can be disrupted by heavy snowfall.

But snow does have its uses. It is an important source of water. When it melts in the mountains, it provides water for streams, **hydroelectric** power plants and **reservoirs**. It also helps protect plants and hibernating animals from the cold winter air.

STORMS AT SEA

The sea never stops moving because the air above it is never still. The wind makes ripples and waves on the sea's surface. As the wind gets stronger, the waves become bigger and very strong winds can whip the surface of the sea into a terrifying mass of spray. Storm waves are powerful and out at sea they may rise higher than 12m. They can pick up huge boulders and throw them far up on the shore. They can even hurl large ships against rocks and smash them.

The largest waves are called **tsunamis** (a Japanese word meaning 'overflowing waves'). These are not caused by wind but by underwater volcanic explosions or earthquakes which cause the sea floor to rise and fall. Tsunamis travel quickly, at up to 800km per hour. Where the sea bed gets shallower, they slow down but become higher. A tsunami can form a wall of water more than 24m high when it approaches shallow water near shore. If a tsunami reaches land, it can swamp large areas and cause terrible damage.

▼ Storms can cause problems for ships at sea.

Wind causes waves which form far out to sea. The wind pushes the water particles which move round and round. Near the coast, where the water is shallow, the sea bed interferes with the movement of the water. Then the top of the wave breaks on to the beach.

HURRICANES, TYPHOONS AND CYCLONES

Violent, whirling storms which begin over warm oceans are known by different names in different parts of the world. In the Caribbean they are called **hurricanes**, in the China Seas **typhoons** and in the Indian Ocean **cyclones**. Storm clouds, rain and howling winds of up to 300km per hour race across the sky, stirring up huge waves on the surface of the sea below.

When one of these tropical storms moves over land, strong winds and heavy rain hit the area for several hours. Fields, even towns may be flooded, trees and crops uprooted and buildings destroyed. Sometimes, many people are killed. Gradually the storm dies down until at last it blows itself out.

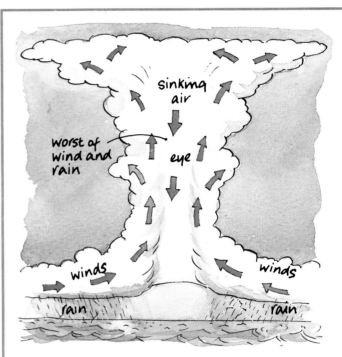

Most tropical storms develop in summer, when the seas and the air above are at their warmest. As the sea heats the air, a current of warm, moist air rises above the water. Winds rush in below this air current and whirl upwards. As they rise, they cool, and the huge amounts of water vapour they contain form towering clouds. At the centre of the storm is a calm area known as the **eye**. In a circle immediately around the eye, the wind and rain are at their fiercest. Although the air in the eye is hotter than in the rest of the storm, it does not rise. Instead, it sinks slowly down to the surface of the sea.

◄ The fierce winds of a tropical storm have blown this plane right out of the sky. It has landed in an area flooded by the storm's heavy rain.

▲ Palm trees battered by the winds of an approaching tropical storm.

▼ This photograph, taken from the American space shuttle *Discovery*, shows the whirling clouds of a hurricane. Right in the centre of the storm you can see the calm 'eye'.

SAND AND DUSTSTORMS

Wind blowing over a sandy area such as a desert or a dry river bed picks up sand and carries it through the air, creating a sandstorm. Most of the sand stays about 51cm above the ground, although some grains can rise to a height of about 2m. During a sandstorm, the sand seems to jump along as the grains bang against each other and then bounce up into the air.

Sandstorms can be a danger to desert travellers. The stinging clouds of sand can clog machinery and reduce visibility. They can also damage crops.

Some desert animals have special ways of protecting themselves against sandstorms. The camel, for instance, can close its nostrils and has a second set of eyelids to cover its eyes.

◀ Dust storms occur where the ground is very dry or has been badly farmed, resulting in bare soil with no vegetation to protect it. Thousands of tonnes of dusty soil are carried high into the air by strong winds and blown away. Dust storms help to cause **soil erosion** and can strip all the fertile earth away from a large area.

TORNADOES

A **tornado** is a violent, twisting, whirlwind which forms over land and is often accompanied by heavy rain, thunder and lightning. It looks like a funnel-shaped cloud reaching downwards from the base of a cumulonimbus cloud. Tornadoes form in warm, moist air where winds blow into each other from opposite directions. A whirling column of hot air is created which spins at tremendous speed until it stretches from the cloud to the ground.

As the whirling column of the tornado hurtles over the ground at speeds of up to 97 km per hour, the strong upward current of air at its centre sucks up or destroys everything in its path.

▲ Tornadoes are the most destructive winds that occur on our planet. They are most common in the USA.

MAKE A WEATHER STATION

This weather station will help you keep track of the weather, just like a real scientist.

RAIN GAUGE

It's easy to measure how much rain falls, with the help of a rain gauge.

You need:
- A flat-bottomed glass jar or bottle
- A plastic funnel with the same diameter as the jar or bottle
- A ruler

Place the funnel in the jar. Use the ruler to measure the amount of rainfall.

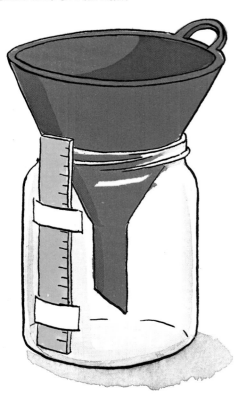

BAROMETER

A **barometer** measures the amount of air pressing down on the Earth. A rise in pressure is a sign of good weather, but if the pressure drops, look out for storms!

You need:
- A jam jar with a wide neck
- A balloon
- Scissors
- A thick rubber band
- A drinking straw
- A needle
- Scotch tape and glue
- A piece of cardboard
- A ruler and a pen
- Plasticine

1 Cut the neck off the balloon. Stretch the rest of the balloon tightly over the neck of the jar. Use the rubber band to hold it in place.

2 Tape the needle to one end of the straw. Glue the other end to the centre of the balloon.

3 Mark off a scale on the cardboard. Push the cardboard into the centre of the plasticine, then place it just behind the point of the needle. As the air pressure changes the balloon will move slightly and the needle will move up and down the scale.

WIND SOCK

A wind sock tells you from which direction the wind is blowing. It will also give you a rough idea of the wind's speed.

You need:
- A piece of lightweight cloth, 1m x 1m
- Scissors
- A needle and thread
- A wire coathanger
- A curtain ring
- Strong card
- A felt pen (with waterproof ink)
- An old broom handle
- Drawing pins
- A garden cane, 60-70 cm
- Strong string
- A compass

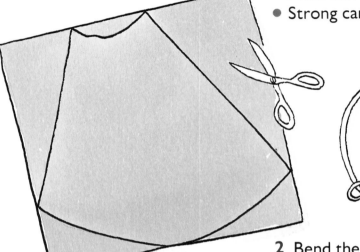

I Cut out a 'sock' shape from your material and sew the straight edges together.

2 Bend the coathanger into a circle. Squeeze the hook until it forms a small ring. Slip the curtain ring on to the wire circle at the side opposite the hook.

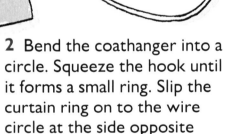

3 Fold the wide curved edge of the sock over the wire circle and stitch it into place. Leave the hook and the curtain ring sticking out.

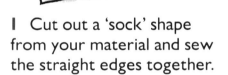

4 Cut out a circle about 30 cm in diameter from the card. Make two slits in the centre of the circle large enough to allow the card to fit tightly on to the broom handle. Write the letters N, E, S, W on the underside of the circle, to act as points of the compass.

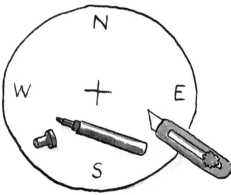

5 Slide the circle on to the broom handle and pin in position.

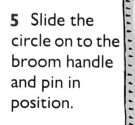

6 Slide the garden cane through the curtain ring and wire hook. Tie the cane firmly to the broom handle.

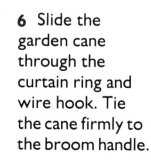

THERMOMETER

A **thermometer** measures the temperature of the air.

You need:
- A glass bottle with a screw top
- Water
- Coloured ink
- A drinking straw
- Plasticine
- A piece of card
- A ruler
- A pen
- Sticky tape

1 Fill the bottle right to the top with water coloured by a little ink.
2 Ask an adult to make a hole (just large enough for the straw) in the screw top.
3 Fix the screw top tightly in position and push the straw through the hole. Put plasticine round the straw.
4 Make a card scale and tape it to the back of the straw.

As the temperature rises and falls, the coloured water will move up and down the straw, giving you a rough guide as to how much hotter or colder the air temperature has become.

Setting up

Dig a hole in the ground for your rain gauge, away from trees and bushes if possible. Your barometer will work indoors or outdoors, but don't place it in the sun. Tie the wind sock to a fence post, or to the roof of a shed or garage. It should be at least 2 m above ground. Keep it away from any trees and buildings that might prevent the wind blowing freely. Your thermometer needs to be in a shady place outdoors.

Check all the measurements two or three times a day. Keep a log book with your results.

me	air pressure		wind direction	temperature	rainfall	remarks
	pressure	trend				
		falling	S.W.	rising	none	cloudy morning
	high	steady	S.W.	rising	5mm	rain at midday, sun trying to break through
8am	average					clear, dry evening
1pm		rising	W.	falling	none	
	average					

SCIENCE AT WORK

Every hour of the day and night, weather stations all round the world are recording facts and figures about the weather. Temperatures, wind direction, wind speed, cloud cover, rainfall and **air pressure** are all measured, and the information transmitted to a national weather office. There, weather scientists, or **meteorologists**, draw up a map called a **synoptic chart**. Each local weather station is marked on this map by a circle. The information it has sent in is marked around it, using coded symbols which are recognised all over the world.

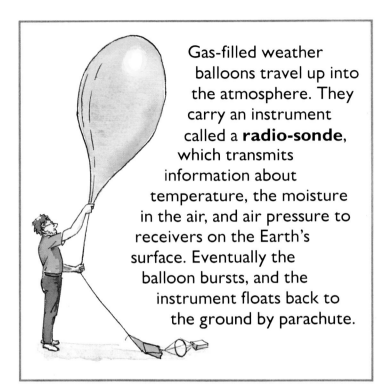

Gas-filled weather balloons travel up into the atmosphere. They carry an instrument called a **radio-sonde**, which transmits information about temperature, the moisture in the air, and air pressure to receivers on the Earth's surface. Eventually the balloon bursts, and the instrument floats back to the ground by parachute.

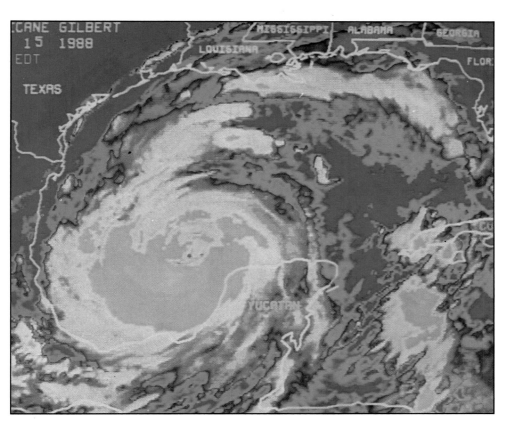

◀ Satellites are especially helpful in detecting hurricanes over tropical oceans. Meteorologists are now more easily able to chart a storm's progress.

▼ Some weather satellites orbit the Earth, moving from Pole to Pole. Others become stationary over a fixed place on the Equator. The television cameras they carry scan the Earth below, then transmit signals to receivers on the Earth's surface. These signals can be changed into pictures.

When the synoptic chart is complete, the information is fed into a computer. The computer then prints out maps which forecast how weather conditions are likely to change in the following days.

Measuring instruments such as weather balloons and satellites have allowed meteorologists to discover many new things about the weather. The use of computers means that they can find out what the weather is like in any part of the world at any given time. The result is more accurate weather forecasting.

◀ Weather satellites take photographs of the Earth from space. These photographs show the cloud cover over different parts of the Earth's surface, and help meteorologists to trace the development and movement of cloud systems.

THE HURRICANE

Father turned off the radio. 'Hurricane warning,' he told them. 'Come on. You know what to do.'

It took them nearly an hour to fasten all the shutters securely and move the garden furniture into the house. By the time they had finished it had started to get dark. A huge mass of iron-grey clouds filled the sky to the east, towering above the mud-coloured sea. The horizon was black, lit only by the distant flicker of lightning. The wind had started to rise, sweeping the dust off the streets. In the distance unfastened doors and shutters banged. Hurricane Dora was about to arrive.

'Everyone downstairs,' ordered Father. The family clattered down into the cellar and sat nervously in the darkened room. They knew there was not long to wait.

By ten o'clock the sky was black. Still no rain had fallen, but the wind had started to tear at the palm trees, bending them almost in two. In the bay below, the little fishing port disappeared in a thick fog of sea spray. Waves began to smash up the beach, spilling water on to the road beyond.

Ten minutes later the full force of the hurricane hit the island. The tidal wave which had been building up across the ocean surged into the bay. As the wave raced towards the land, it was pushed into the narrow space between the cliffs on either side of the bay, and it began to rise. By the time it reached the beach, the wall of water was over five metres high. It was unstoppable. It surged over the sand and crashed into the little painted wooden houses, sweeping them away like litter.

A fishing boat was somehow, miraculously, lifted out of the bay, carried over the town and dropped gently on to the roof of the fire station. There it remained, trapped by a mass of splintered timbers. An advertising board as big as a house whirled through the air like a playing card.

The noise of the wind was like the roar of a dozen aeroplane engines all revving up together. The wind had risen to about two hundred and forty kilometres an hour. It was strong enough to pick up humans like pieces of straw and whirl them away. At that speed it could even knock down the side of a house.

Hurricane Dora tore across the island, uprooting large trees and tossing them around like paper darts. She ripped the soil from the fields and churned it into brown mist. And then came the rain. The drops were enormous. It sounded as if someone was emptying a never-ending stream of gravel over the house.

Within minutes the ground had become a quagmire. Every hollow in the ground was filled with water. Water spilled out of the hollows and began to run downhill. Tracks became streams. Streams became torrents. The water raced downwards trying to reach the sea. It carved at the land, tearing out mud, boulders and trees. The river rose and within minutes had burst its banks. Dark brown water spilled out over the countryside.

The family, safe in their cellar, huddled together and listened to Dora's progress. Apart from an uncanny half hour of silence, when the eye of the hurricane passed over them, the wind and rain battered at the house for twelve hours.

Then, at last, Hurricane Dora had gone. The family climbed stiffly up the stairs and went outside. They gasped at the devastation they saw. Their garden had disappeared. In its place was a crazy chaos of smashed trees, upturned cars and bits of other people's houses. They turned and looked at their own house. The pink paint was covered with marks caused by flying objects. Charlotte pointed at the roof. Only three tiles remained in place.

Laura ran to the bottom of the garden and looked down on to the little fishing port below. 'Oh, no!' she gasped in horror. The rest of them peered down. The stone jetty was all that remained of the town. The houses had vanished. A few people had returned from their refuges in the hills and were walking about, searching for the remains of their homes.

'It will all be rebuilt,' Father assured them. 'This isn't the first hurricane to hit the island, and it won't be the last.'

'Yes,' added Mother. 'And thanks to the hurricane warning on the radio, it's unlikely that anyone was hurt. Everyone will have got to the hills in plenty of time.'

'Come on,' said Father. 'We've got a lot of tidying up to do. Let's get to work.'

From down below in the village came the sound of hammering, as people began to build new wooden houses.

TRUE OR FALSE?

Which of these facts are true and which ones are false?
If you have read this book carefully, you will know the answers.

A rainbow is a full circle of colour.

2 We always hear thunder before we see lightning.

3 The atmosphere is a thin blanket of air which surrounds the Earth.

4 Hailstones fall from any type of cloud.

5 Tsunami is another word for tornado.

6 Scientists who study weather are called meteorologists.

7 A snowfall of as little as 10 cm is enough to block roads.

8 An avalanche is caused by the movement of waves.

9 At the centre of a hurricane is a calm area known as the 'eye'.

10 The driest place in the world is Mount Wai-'ale-'ale in Hawaii.

11 Tornadoes emerge only from cumulonimbus clouds.

12 The strong winds of a dust storm can strip the ground of soil.

13 A thermometer measures air pressure.

GLOSSARY

Active is the word used to describe a live volcano while it is erupting.

Air mass is a huge area of air with the same temperature throughout.

Air pressure is the phrase used to describe the force of the air pushing down on the Earth. The amount of air pressure varies from place to place and it can change from day to day. Rising air pressure usually means that good weather is on the way; falling air pressure usually means that the weather will turn unpleasant.

Antennae are the parts of an insect's body which it uses for touching and feeling. Antennae are positioned on an insect's head.

Atmosphere is the thin blanket of air that surrounds the Earth.

Avalanche is a sudden fall of snow and ice down a steep slope. Avalanches can be caused by disturbances such as heavy winds, earth tremors and explosions. They can be very dangerous to people and animals who may be in their way.

Baleen is horn-like material made of keratin, the same substance as hair and nails. Instead of teeth, some types of whale have a series of baleen plates in their mouth.

Barometer is an instrument used to measure air pressure.

Blubber is a layer of fat under the skin. Many animals who live in cold areas of the world have blubber to help keep themselves warm.

Bow is the name given to the front or 'fore-end' of a boat or ship.

Bromeliads are members of a large family of plants, most of which grow in the tropical rainforests of Central and South America. Most bromeliads are epiphytes, and have long, sword-shaped leaves.

Caldera is the huge round crater which forms when the cone of a live volcano collapses inward.

Colonisation means sending people from one area of a country to another, or from one country to another, so that they can build homes and form a new town or settlement elsewhere.

Cone is the mountain which builds up around a volcano. It is made up of hardened lava, as well as the ash and cinders which are thrown out of the volcano during an explosion.

Core is the name given to the centre of the Earth. It is divided into the outer core, which is made up of hot, liquid metals, and the inner core, which is solid iron.

Crater is the hole found at the top of a volcano's vent. It widens each time the volcano erupts.

Crust is the name given to the Earth's thin surface layer. It is made up of huge, thick slabs of rock called plates which float on the hot, liquid rock of the mantle, the next layer down.

Cumulonimbus is the name of a huge thundercloud which brings heavy rain, snow or hail. Cumulonimbus clouds often stretch high into the atmosphere.

Cyclone is the word used in the area of the Indian Ocean to describe a tropical storm.

Dormant is the word used to describe a live volcano while it is not erupting.

Epiphytes are plants which grow on other plants and take their food and water from the air. Epiphytes do not harm the plants that they grow on, unlike parasites, which harm their 'hosts'.

Evergreens are trees which have green leaves all year round. They do shed their old leaves, but they form new ones first.

Extinction means 'dying out'. A species of animal or plant becomes extinct when every one of its kind has died. Species usually become extinct because their habitat is destroyed and they have lost their source of food, although some animals may have become extinct because they have been killed off by humans.

Eye is the name given to the calm area in the centre of a hurricane.

Flash flood is a severe flood which occurs after sudden, very heavy rain has caused rivers to burst their banks.

Flippers are limbs used by animals such as seals, who spend all or most of their lives in water, to help them swim well.

Flora and fauna is a phrase used to describe the plant and animal species found in a particular area.

Front is the name given to the edge of an air mass.

Geothermal energy is energy which is obtained from the volcanic areas or 'hot zones' below the surface of the Earth.

Geyser is a natural underground spring which shoots up jets of steam on to the surface.

Glacier is the name given to a slowly moving river of ice.

Global warming and the **greenhouse effect** are phrases used to describe the warming of the Earth caused by gases which have been released into the atmosphere. These gases trap heat on Earth, which has come from the Sun, and so the Earth warms up. Nobody is quite sure what the final effect will be, but if the Earth continues to warm up, the ice at the Poles will begin to melt. This will make the sea levels rise and, eventually, large areas of land could disappear underwater.

Habitat is the word used to describe the natural home of a plant, animal, insect or person.

Hot springs are found underground. The warm water they contain bubbles up to the surface.

Hotspot is an area of fierce heat in the Earth's mantle (see separate entry) where magma bubbles up to the surface and forms a volcano.

Hull is the name given to the body or frame of a ship.

Hurricane is the word used in the area of the Caribbean to describe a tropical storm.

Huskies are dogs used in the Arctic for pulling sledges across the ice.

Hydroelectricity is electricity which is produced by using water power.

Ice sheet is a thick layer of ice which extends over a vast area.

Ice shelf is a great ledge of ice which projects from the edge of an ice sheet.

Irregular iceberg is the name used to describe an iceberg which does not have a regular shape.

Krill are small, shrimp-like

creatures. In the summer, they are found in huge swarms in the seas around Antarctica. They are eaten by baleen whales.

Lava is the name given to magma from inside the Earth when it escapes on to the Earth's surface.

Lemurs are monkey-like animals which are found on the island of Madagascar. Most lemurs live in trees, and some are active only at night.

Loggers are people who are employed to cut down trees.

Magma is hot, liquid rock found inside the Earth, in the layer called the mantle.

Mantle is the layer inside the Earth, below the crust. It is made up of hot, liquid rock called magma.

Meteorologist is a scientist who studies the weather.

Minerals are substances, other than plants, which can be dug from the ground. Minerals are solid, non-living substances that are needed by all living things in order to survive and grow.

Moult means to lose feathers or hair. Once a year, a number of animals and birds moult. Their old feathers or hair fall out, to be replaced by new growth underneath.

Ozone layer is the name given to the layer of Earth's atmosphere which protects us from the dangerous effects of the Sun's ultraviolet rays.

Pahoehoe is the name given to the wrinkled, rope-like surface produced by runny lava as it cools and hardens.

Plantation is a large area of land used for the growing of a particular crop.

Plates are huge, thick slabs

of rock which make up the Earth's crust.

Polar icecap is the name of the ice sheet which covers most of Antarctica.

Pollution is the waste and rubbish that is dumped by humans. 'To pollute' means 'to make dirty'. Humans are making the planet 'dirty' by introducing harmful sub-stances into the environment in the form of 'pollution'. These substances often cause great damage to plants and animals.

Pumice is a very light type of rock which can float in water. It is formed when lava cools very quickly.

Pygmy is the word used to describe a group of native African people who live in the tropical rainforests, and a group of people who live in parts of Asia. Pygmies are usually between 1.2 and 1.4m tall.

Radio-sonde is a special instrument which is carried up into the atmosphere on a weather balloon. It is able to transmit information about temperature, air pressure and the amount of moisture in the air to receivers on the Earth's surface.

Reforestation means planting trees over a bare area of ground which was once covered by forest.

Reservoir is a large, artificial lake where water is stored before being treated and piped into people's homes.

Return stroke is the movement of a flash of lightning from the ground back up to the cloud from which it came. It is the bright light of the return stroke that we actually see.

Ring of Fire is the name given to the area around the Pacific Ocean where a large number of the world's live volcanoes are found.

Rounded iceberg is an iceberg whose edges have been softened by the effects of wind and waves, and is, therefore, rounded in shape.

Seismometer is a special instrument which can pinpoint the position of rising magma. It is used by scientists to help predict where and when a volcano is going to erupt.

Soil erosion is the stripping away of the top, fertile layer of soil. This can be caused by weather conditions, such as strong winds and heavy floods.

Species is the word used to describe a group of animals or plants which are alike in certain ways.

Synoptic chart is a type of weather map. It shows readings from every one of a country's weather stations, and uses coded numbers, signs and symbols that are recognised by meteorologists all over the world.

Tabular iceberg is the name used to describe huge, flat icebergs with table-like tops.

Tapir is a type of mammal which looks like a giant pig but is in fact related to the rhinoceros.

Thermometer is an instrument used to measure air temperature.

Tiltmeter is an instrument which measures the amount of tilt in the ground caused by magma pushing up from underground and making the sides of a volcano swell. This information can help scientists predict where an eruption will occur.

Tornado is a violent, twisting whirlwind which forms over land. It looks like a funnel-shaped cloud extending down from the base of a cumulonimbus cloud. It spins at tremendous speed over the ground and causes serious damage to land, property, animals and people.

Tropical hardwood is wood obtained from many tropical rainforest trees. Mahogany, ebony, teak and rosewood are all tropical hardwoods.

Tsunami is the name given to the huge wave caused by underwater volcanic explosions or earthquakes. If a tsunami reaches land, it can cause terrible damage.

Typhoon is the word used in the area of the China Seas to describe a tropical storm.

Ultraviolet radiation is the harmful effect caused by the Sun's ultraviolet rays. Ultraviolet is the part of sunlight which causes a suntan, but it also causes skin cancer. These problems will increase if the ozone layer is damaged any further and is no longer able to protect us from these rays.

Vent is an opening in a volcano through which magma flows. The main vent is usually in the centre of a volcano, but sometimes there are vents in the sides of volcanoes too.

Volcanic ash is the name given to the smallest pieces of rock thrown out of a volcano when it erupts.

Volcanic bombs are the largest pieces of rock thrown out of a volcano.

Volcanic plug is the piece of solid lava which remains after weather has worn away a volcano's cone over a period of thousands of years.

INDEX

NOTES